EASY
GUITAR
WITH NOTES & TAB

CROSBY, STILLS & NASH
EASY GUITAR COLLECTION

Cover photo © Michael Putland / Retna Ltd.

ISBN 978-1-4234-9203-0

HAL•LEONARD®
CORPORATION
7777 W. BLUEMOUND RD. P.O. BOX 13819 MILWAUKEE, WI 53213

Visit Hal Leonard Online at
www.halleonard.com

STRUM AND PICK PATTERNS

This chart contains the suggested strum and pick patterns that are referred to by number at the beginning
of each song in this book. The symbols ⊓ and ∨ in the strum patterns refer to down and up strokes, respectively.
The letters in the pick patterns indicate which right-hand fingers play which strings.

p = thumb
i = index finger
m = middle finger
a = ring finger

For example; Pick Pattern 2
is played: thumb - index - middle - ring

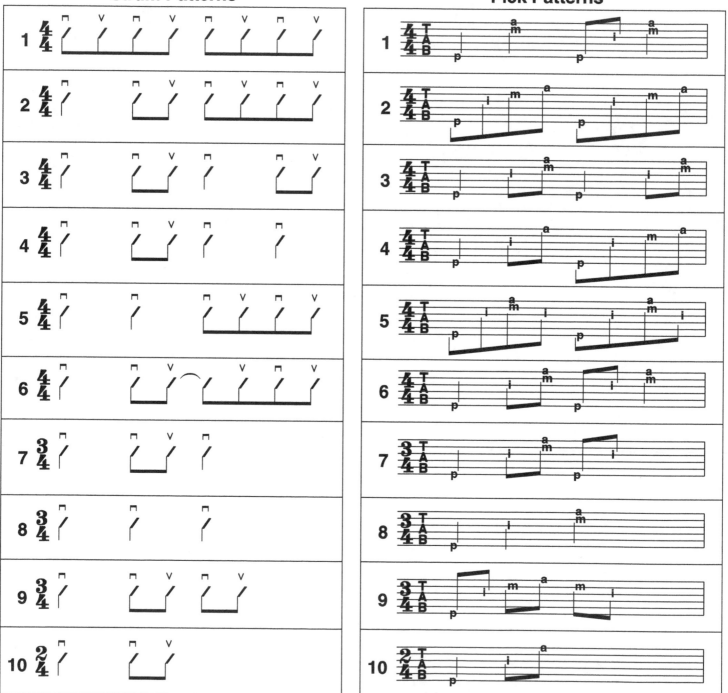

Strum Patterns   Pick Patterns

You can use the 3/4 Strum and Pick Patterns in songs written in compound meter (6/8, 9/8, 12/8, etc.).
For example, you can accompany a song in 6/8 by playing the 3/4 pattern twice in each measure.
The 4/4 Strum and Pick Patterns can be used for songs written in cut time (¢) by doubling the note
time values in the patterns. Each pattern would therefore last two measures in cut time.

Carry Me

Words and Music by David Crosby

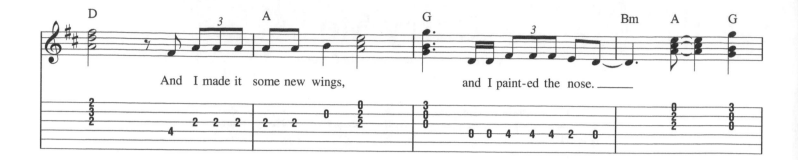

And I made it some new wings, and I paint-ed the nose. _____

And I wished so hard _____ up in the air _____ I rose, _____ sing-in', _

Chorus

_____ "Car - ry me. Car - ry me, _ yeah. Car - ry me _ a - bove the world. _____

Car - ry me, _ oo, _ oo, oo, car - ry me, _____ car - ry me." _

Verse

2. And I once loved a _____ girl, and she was young-er than me.

Her par-ents kept her locked up in their life, _ and she was cry-ing at night. She was wish-ing she could _

_ be free. _____ Course, I most-ly re-mem-ber her laugh-ing,

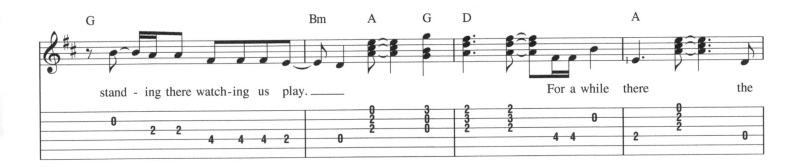

stand - ing there watch-ing us play. _____ For a while there the

Chorus

mu - sic would take her a-way and she'd be sing-in', "Car-ry me, _ car - ry me, yeah.

Car - ry me _ a-bove this world. _ Car - ry me, _ yeah. _ Car - ry me, _ oo. _____

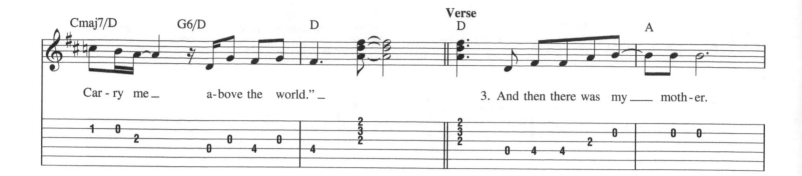

Car-ry me _ a-bove the world." _   3. And then there was my ___ moth-er.

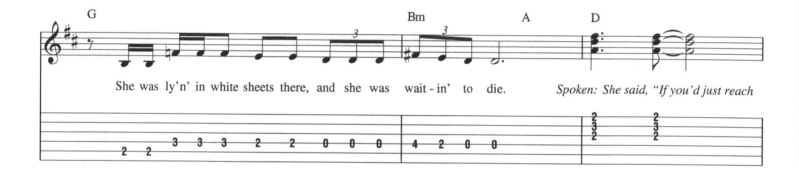

She was ly'n' in white sheets there, and she was wait-in' to die.   *Spoken: She said, "If you'd just reach*

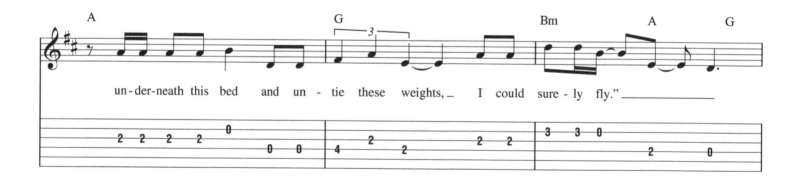

un-der-neath this bed   and un - tie these weights, _   I could sure - ly fly." _____

She's still smil-ing, but she's tired. _____   She'd like to hear _ that last bell ring. _

You know if she still could, she — would stand up and she could sing. —

Chorus

Sing - in, "Car - ry me, — oh, car - ry me, ——— oo. ——— Car - ry me — a-bove the world. —

— Oo, — car - ry me, — oo, ——— car - ry me, yeah." — Mm. —

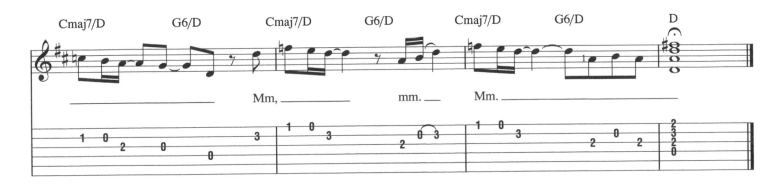

——————————— Mm, ——————— mm. — Mm. ———————

Change Partners

Words and Music by Stephen Stills

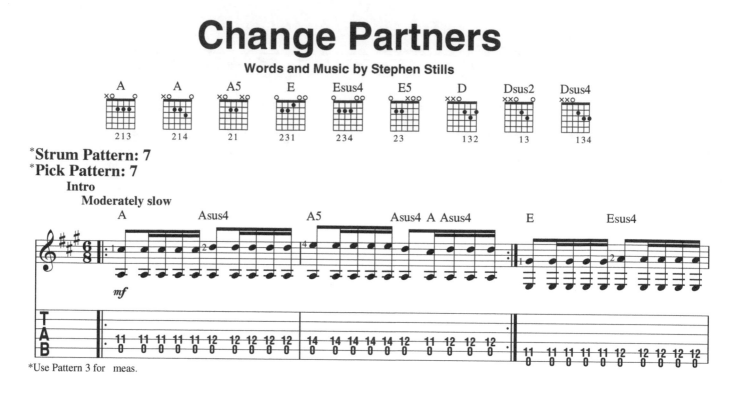

*Strum Pattern: 7
*Pick Pattern: 7

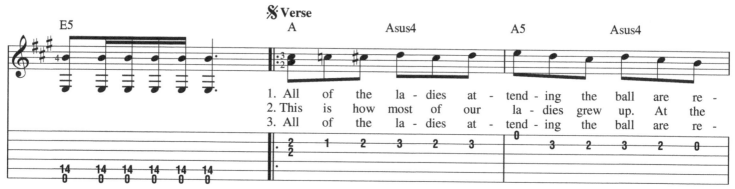

*Use Pattern 3 for meas.

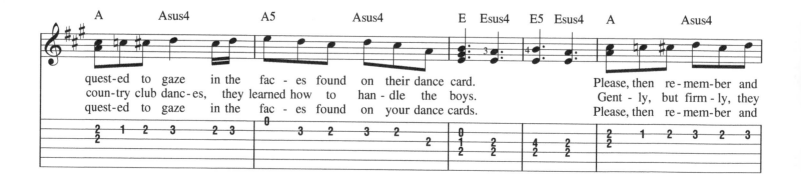

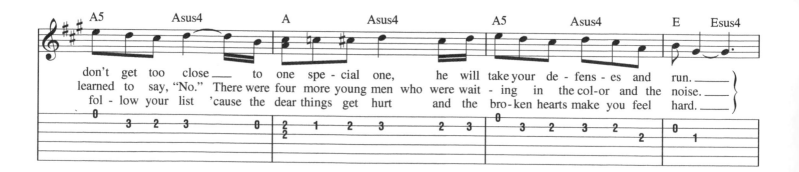

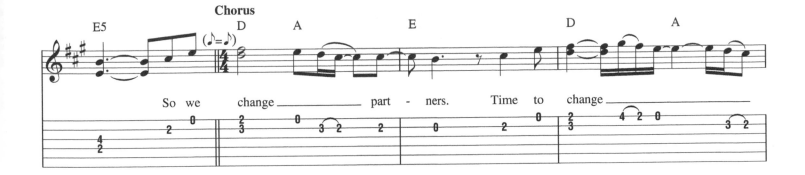

Chorus

So we change _____ part - ners. Time to change _____

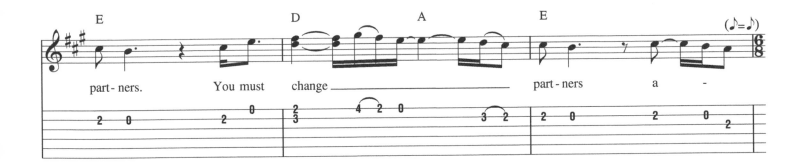

part - ners. You must change _____ part - ners a -

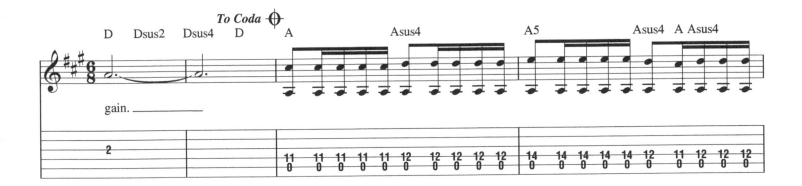

To Coda ⊕

gain. _____

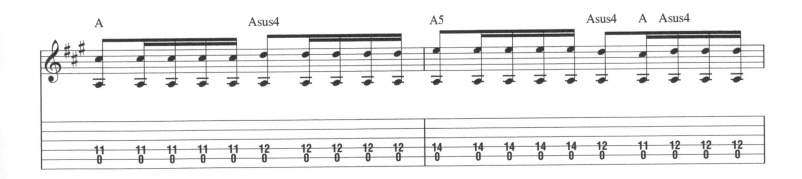

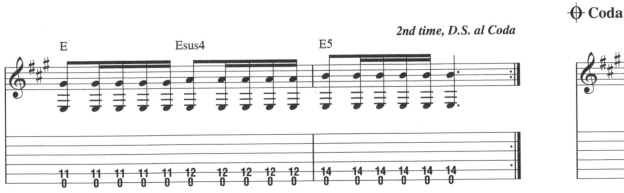

2nd time, D.S. al Coda

⊕ **Coda**

Chicago

Words and Music by Graham Nash

Strum Pattern: 1, 3
Pick Pattern: 3, 5

Intro
Moderately slow, in 2

1. So your broth-er's bound and gagged, and they

chained him to a chair. Won't you please come to Chi-ca-go just to sing?

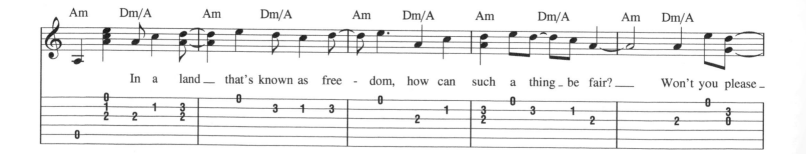

In a land that's known as free-dom, how can such a thing be fair? Won't you please

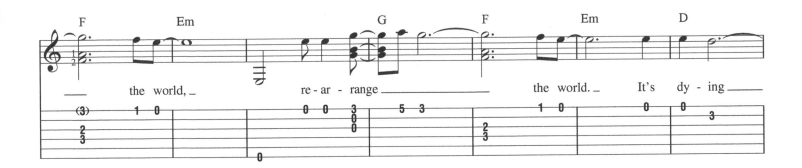

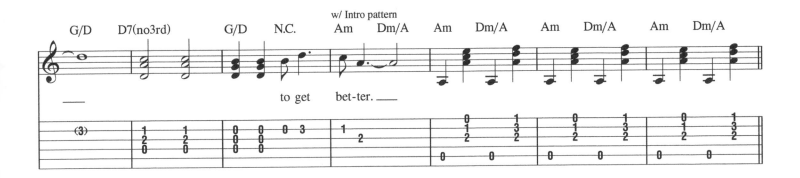

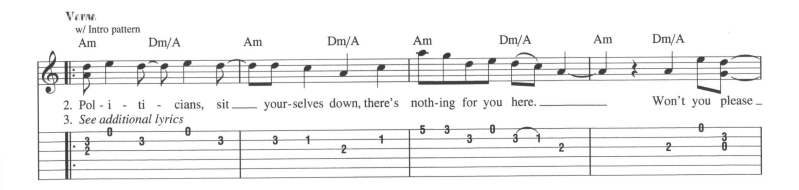

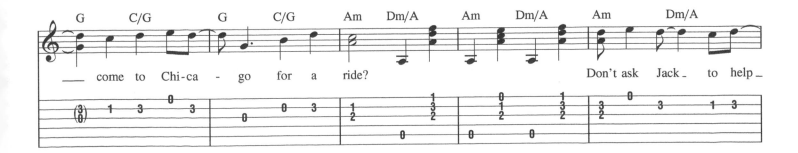

you 'cause he'll turn the oth - er ear. ___ Won't you please __ come to Chi - ca - go or else

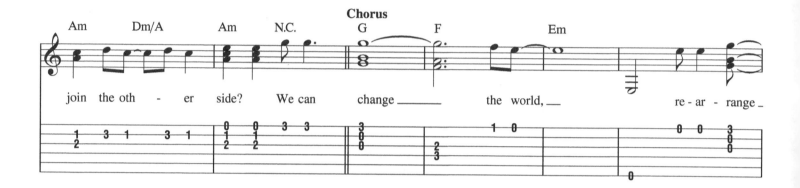

Chorus

join the oth - er side? We can change _____ the world, __ re - ar - range __

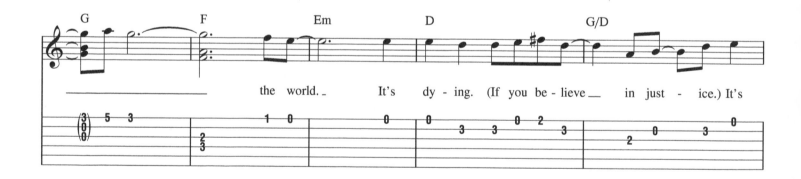

_____ the world. __ It's dy - ing. (If you be - lieve __ in just - ice.) It's

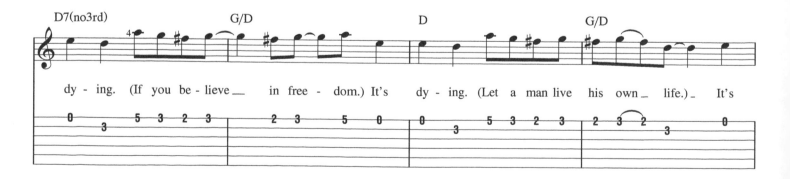

dy - ing. (If you be - lieve __ in free - dom.) It's dy - ing. (Let a man live his own __ life.) __ It's

dy - ing. (Rules _ and reg - u - la - tions, who needs them?)

O - pen up _ the door! _____

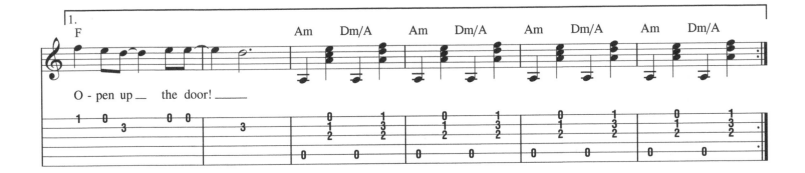

O - pen up _ the door! _____

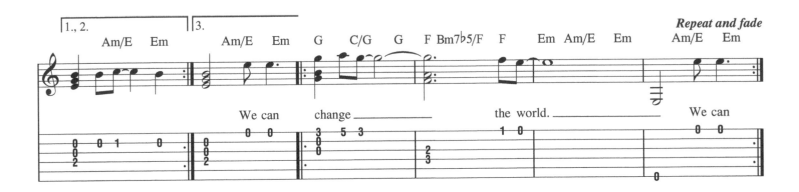

We can change _____ the world. _____ We can

Additional Lyrics

3. Somehow people must be free,
   I hope the day comes soon.
   Won't you please come to Chicago?
   Show your face.
   From the bottom of the ocean
   To the mountains of the moon.
   Won't you please come to Chicago?
   No one else can take your place.

Got It Made

Words and Music by Stephen Stills and Neil Young

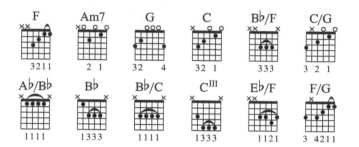

Strum Pattern: 3
Pick Pattern: 3

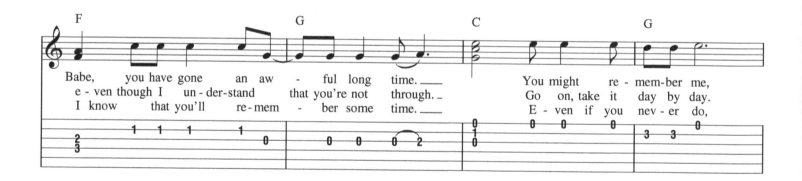

fi - nal - ize ___ your last trade? ___ You ___ are the on - ly one _____ I've ev - er

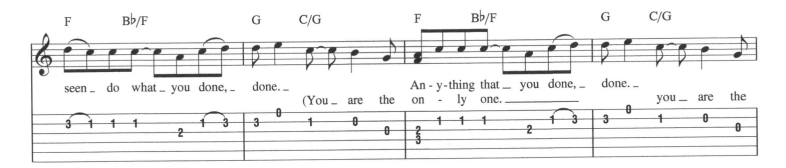

seen ___ do what ___ you done, ___ done. ___
(You ___ are the on - ly one. _____

An - y-thing that ___ you done, ___ done.
you ___ are the

To Coda

Interlude

You are the on - ly one. Don't put me un-der your gun. _____
on - ly one.) _____

Bridge

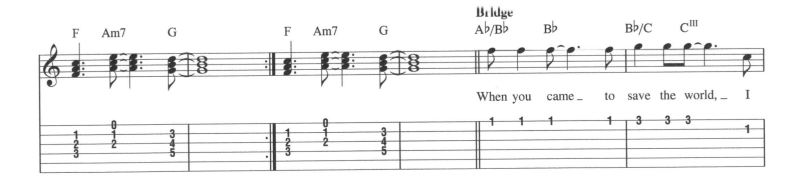

When you came ___ to save the world, ___ I

caused your dreams ___ to fade. ___ I could-n't do ___ what you did, ___ and rained on your pa - rade. ___

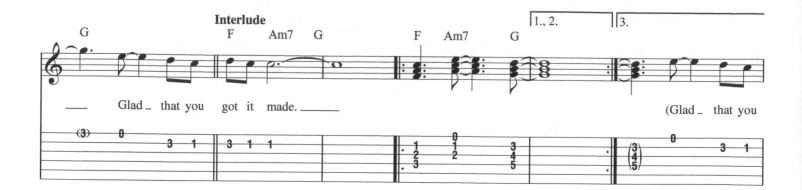

Glad __ that you got it made. _____ (Glad __ that you

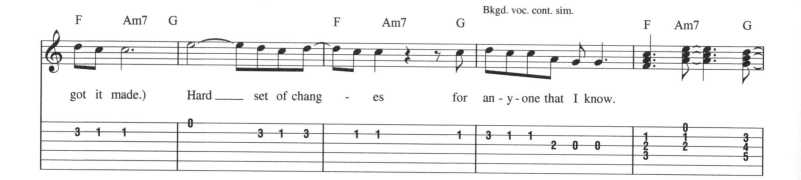

got it made.) Hard _____ set of chang - es for an - y - one that I know.

You're gon - na make __ it, make __ it, make __ it bet - ter for you __ and me and an - y - one else

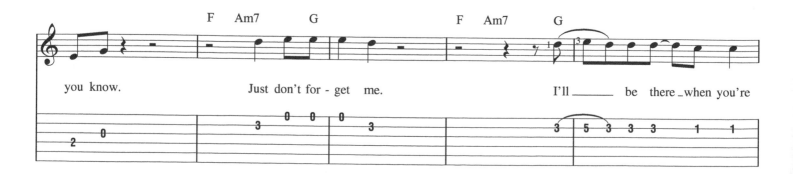

you know. Just don't for - get me. I'll _____ be there __ when you're

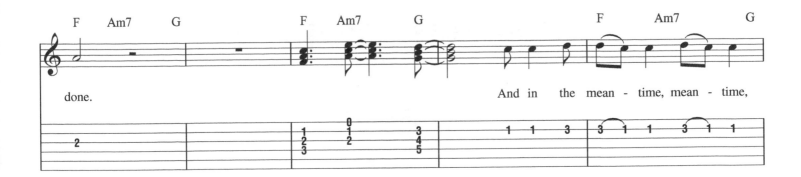

done.

And in the mean - time, mean - time,

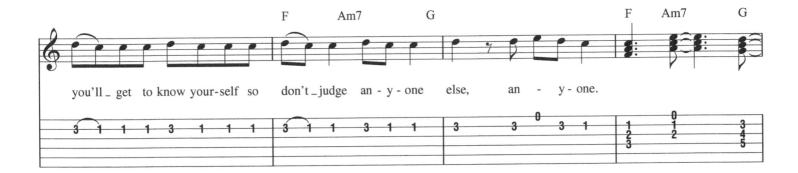

you'll _ get to know your-self so don't _ judge an - y - one else, an - y - one.

⊕ **Coda**

D.S. al Coda

Interlude

No. _____

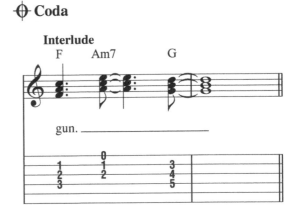

gun. _____

Outro

Repeat and fade

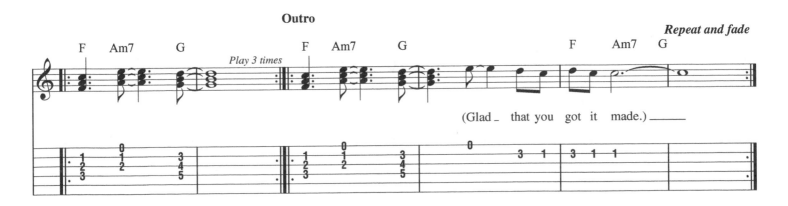

(Glad _ that you got it made.) _____

Helplessly Hoping

Words and Music by Stephen Stills

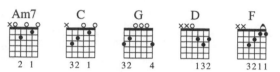

Strum Pattern: 3, 4
Pick Pattern: 3, 4

Intro
Moderately slow

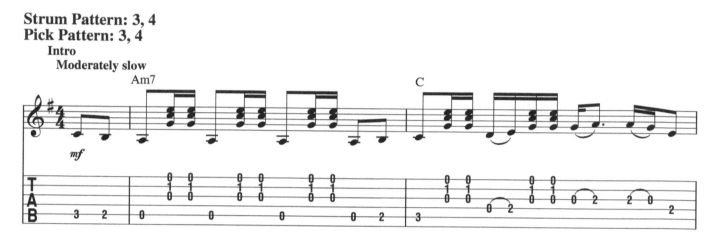

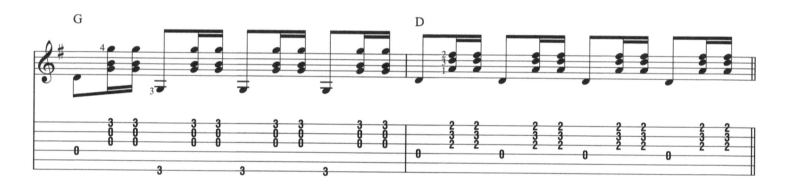

Verse

1. Help - less - ly hop - ing her har - le - quin hov - ers near - by, a - wait - ing a

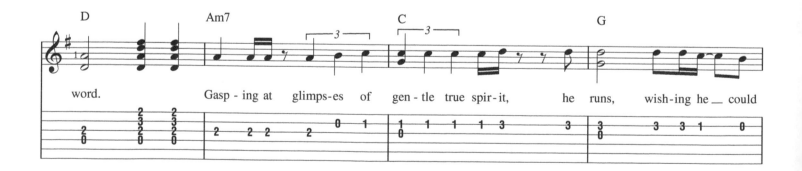

word. Gasp - ing at glimps - es of gen - tle true spir - it, he runs, wish-ing he __ could

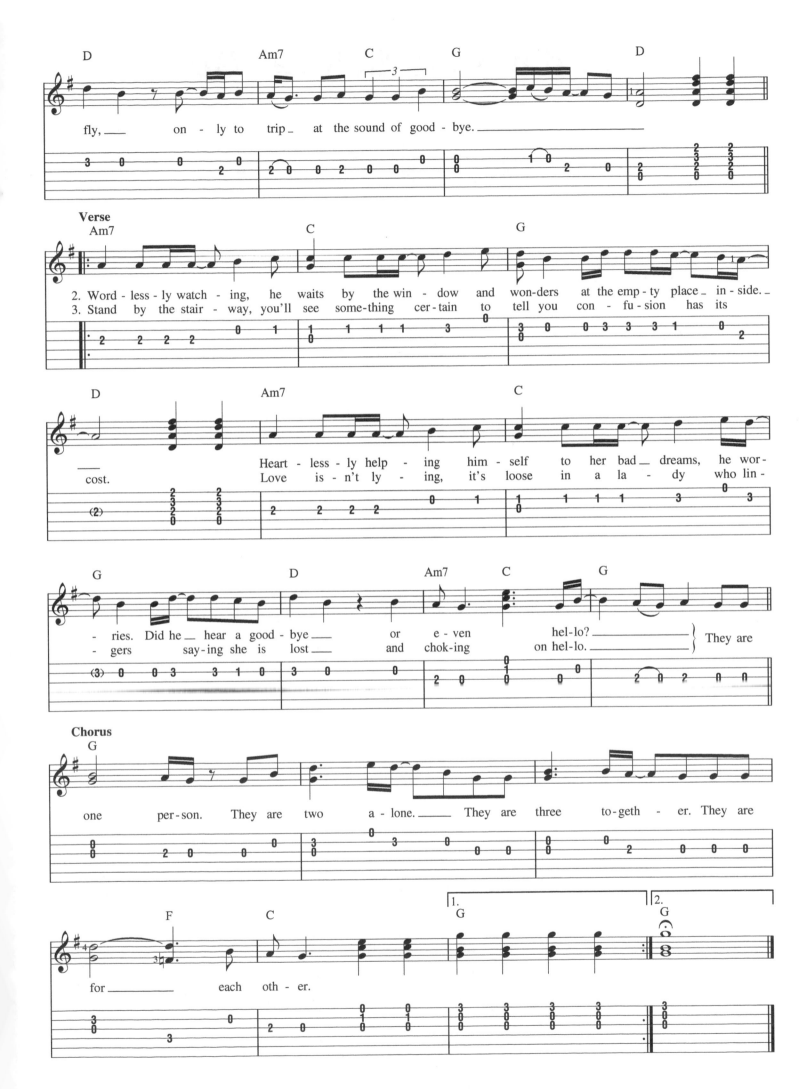

Just a Song Before I Go

Words and Music by Graham Nash

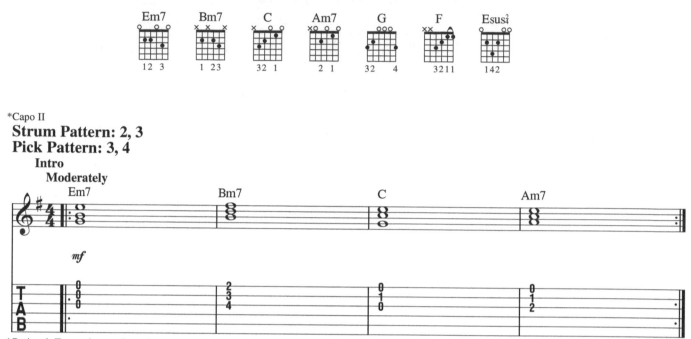

*Capo II

Strum Pattern: 2, 3
Pick Pattern: 3, 4

*Optional: To match recording, place capo at 2nd fret.

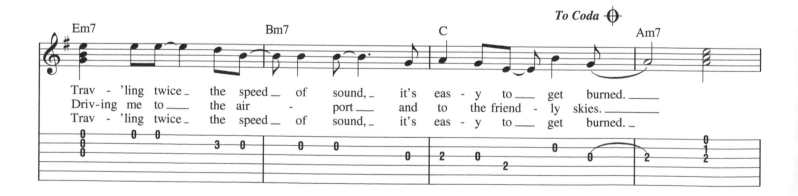

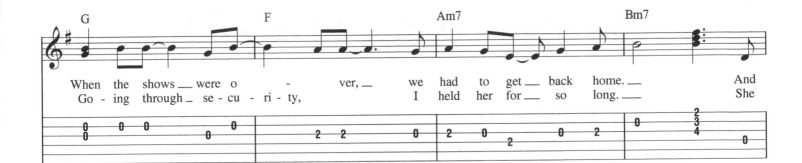

When the shows __ were o - ver, __ we had to get __ back home. __ And

Go - ing through __ se - cu - ri - ty, I held her for __ so long. __ She

1.

when we o - pened up the door, I had to be a - lone. 2. She

fi - n'lly looked __ at me

2. **Guitar Solo**

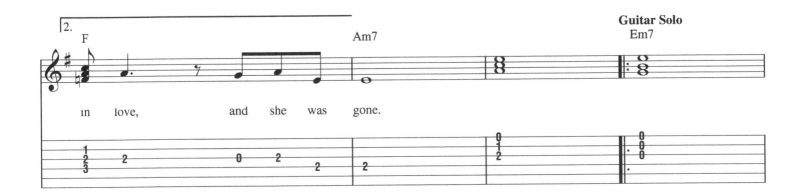

in love, and she was gone.

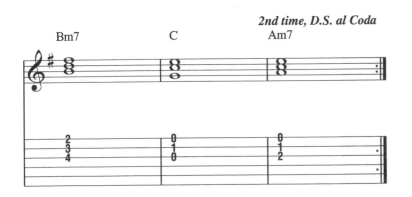

2nd time, D.S. al Coda

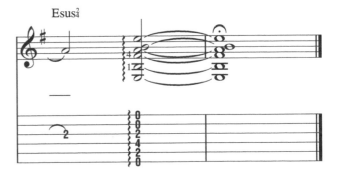

Coda

Love the One You're With

Words and Music by Stephen Stills

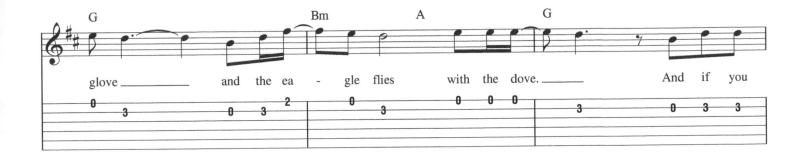

glove _____ and the ea - gle flies with the dove. _____ And if you

can't be with the one __ you love, __ hon-ey, love the one you're with.

Chorus
w/ Intro figure, 2 times

Love the one you're with.

Love the one you're with. Love the one you're with. 2. Don't be an -

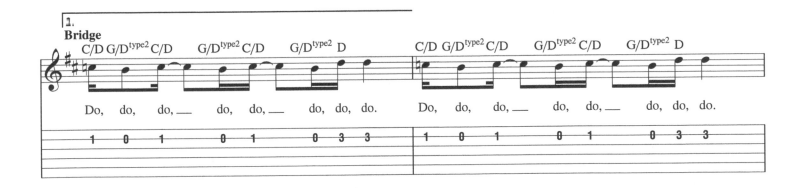

1.
Bridge

Do, do, do, __ do, do, __ do, do, do. Do, do, do, __ do, do, __ do, do, do.

Do, do, do, __ do, do, __ do, do, do. Do, do, do, __ do, do, do.

Organ Solo

Ah. _____

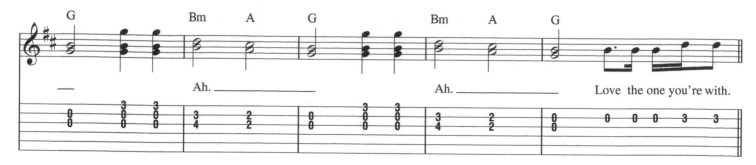

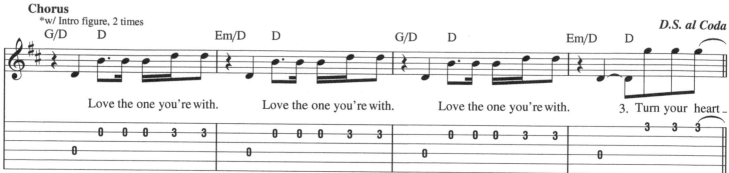

Chorus
*w/ Intro figure, 2 times

D.S. al Coda

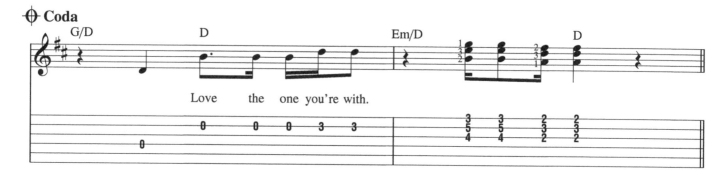

*Optional

Coda

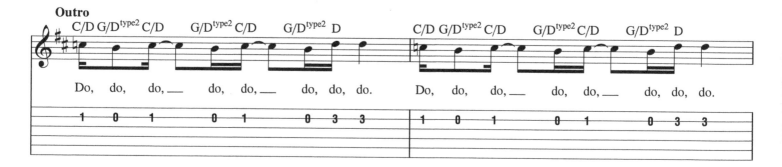

Outro

Additional Lyrics

2. Don't be angry, don't be sad,
   And don't sit cryin' over good times you had.
   There's a girl right next to you
   And she's just waitin' for somethin' to do.

3. Turn your heartache right into joy.
   She is a girl, and you're a boy.
   Get it together, make it nice.
   Ain't gonna need any more advice.

Marrakesh Express

Words and Music by Graham Nash

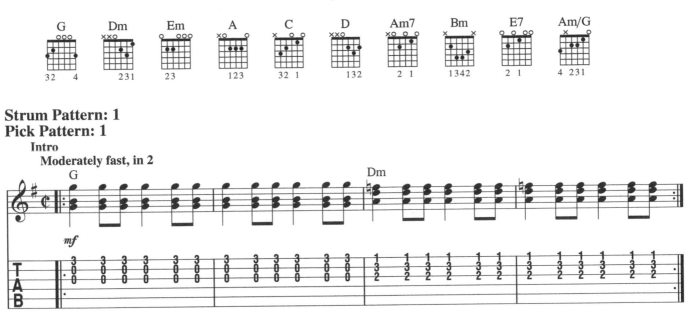

Strum Pattern: 1
Pick Pattern: 1

Intro
Moderately fast, in 2

Verse

1. Look - ing at the world through the sun - set in your eyes,
2. Sweep - ing cob - webs from the edg - es of my mind,
3. Take the train from Ca - sa - blan - ca go - ing south,

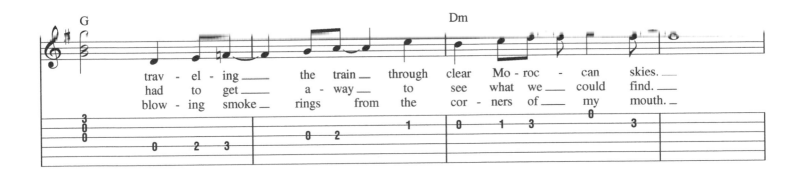

trav - el - ing the train through clear Mo - roc - can skies.
had to get a - way to see what we could find.
blow - ing smoke rings from the cor - ners of my mouth.

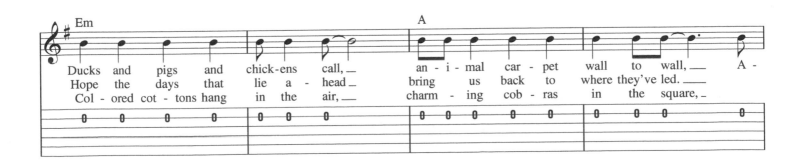

Ducks and pigs and chick - ens call, an - i - mal car - pet wall to wall, A -
Hope the days that lie a - head bring us back to where they've led.
Col - ored cot - tons hang in the air, charm - ing cob - ras in the square,

mer - i - can la - dies five - foot tall in blue.
Lis - ten not to what's been said to you.
striped djel - leb - as we can wear at home. Well, let me hear you now.

Pre-Chorus

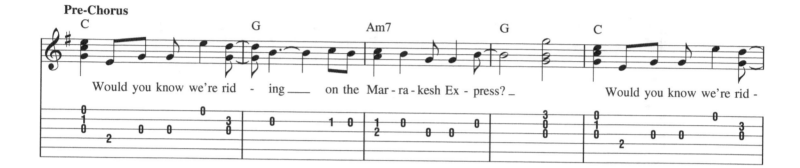

Would you know we're rid - ing ___ on the Mar - ra - kesh Ex - press? ___ Would you know we're rid -

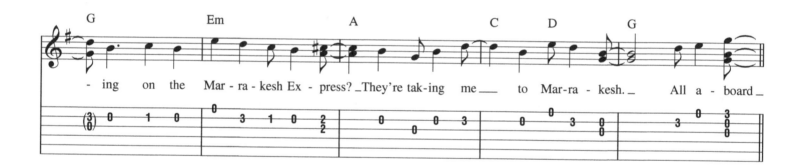

- ing on the Mar - ra - kesh Ex - press? ___ They're tak - ing me ___ to Mar - ra - kesh. ___ All a - board ___

Chorus

___ that train. ___ All a - board ___ that train. ___

Bridge

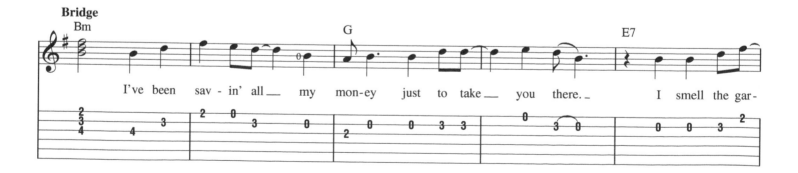

I've been sav - in' all ___ my mon - ey just to take ___ you there. ___ I smell the gar -

-den in __ your hair. _____

Coda

Pre-Chorus

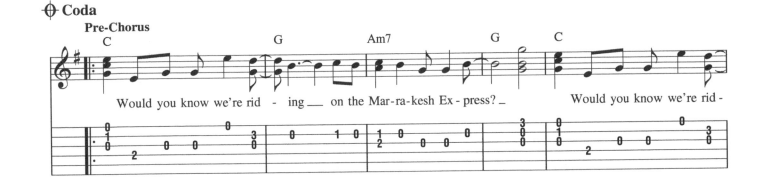

Would you know we're rid - ing __ on the Mar-ra-kesh Ex - press? __ Would you know we're rid-

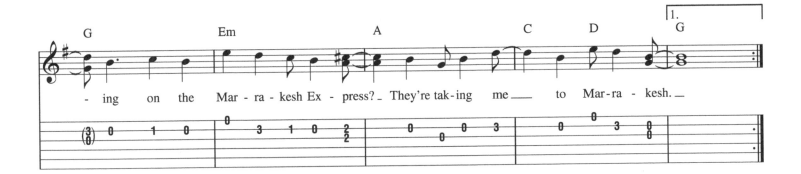

-ing on the Mar - ra - kesh Ex - press? __ They're tak-ing me __ to Mar-ra - kesh. __

Outro-Chorus

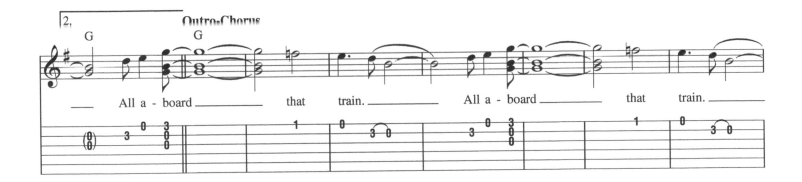

__ All a - board _____ that train. __ All a - board _____ that train. __

Repeat and fade

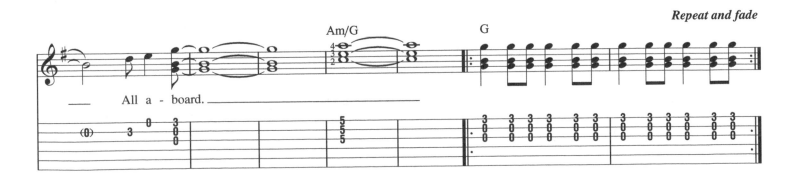

__ All a - board. _____

Our House

Words and Music by Graham Nash

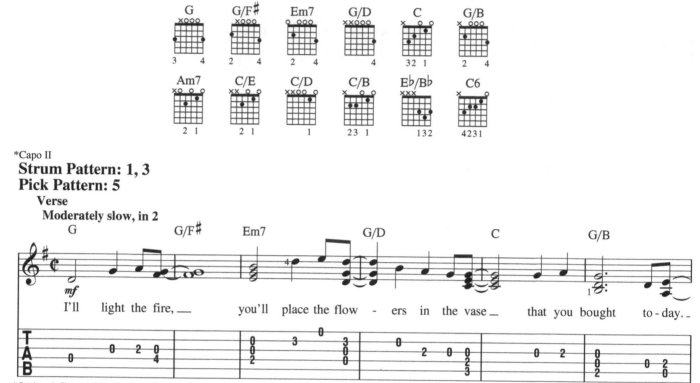

*Capo II

Strum Pattern: 1, 3
Pick Pattern: 5

Verse
Moderately slow, in 2

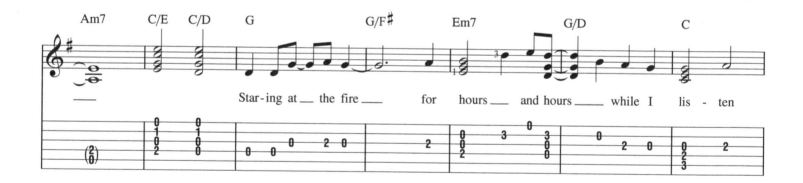

I'll light the fire, ___ you'll place the flow - ers in the vase ___ that you bought to - day.

*Optional: To match recording, place capo at 2nd fret.

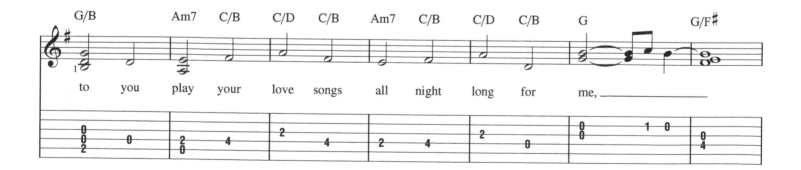

___ Star-ing at ___ the fire ___ for hours ___ and hours ___ while I lis - ten

to you play your love songs all night long for me, ___

on - ly for _ me. _____ 2. Come to me now _ and rest your head _ for just _

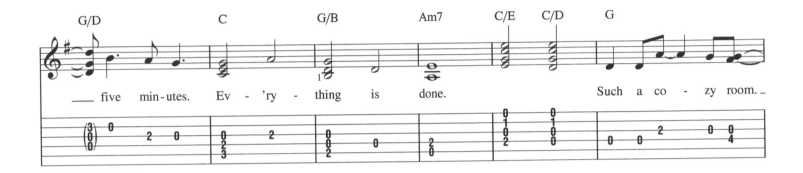

_ five min - utes. Ev - 'ry - thing is done. Such a co - zy room. _

_ The win - dows are il - lu - mi - nat - ed by the eve - ning sun - shine through them

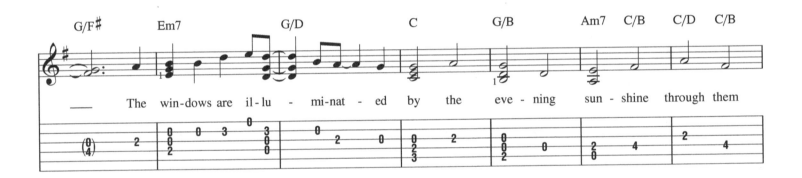

fier - y gems for you, _____ on - ly for _ you. _____

Chorus

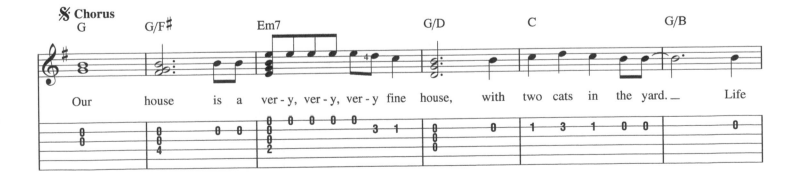

Our house is a ver - y, ver - y, ver - y fine house, with two cats in the yard. _ Life

used to be ___ so hard. ___ Now ev-'ry-thing ___ is eas - y 'cause of you ___

To Coda ⊕
Interlude

and our... La, la, la, la, la, la, la, ___ la, la, la, la, ___ la, la, la, la,

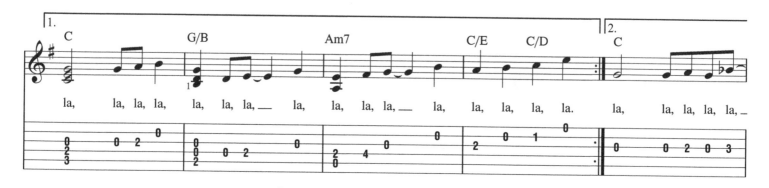

la, la, la, la, la, la, la, ___ la, la, la, la, ___ la, la, la, la. la, la, la, la, la, ___

⊕ **Coda**

D.S. al Coda

Outro-Verse
Slowly

___ la, la, la. I'll light the fire, ___ while you place the flow-

-ers in the vase ___ that you bought ___ to - day. ___

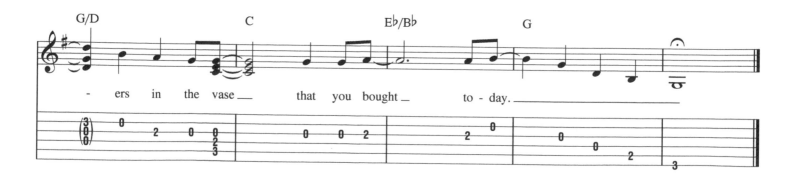

Teach Your Children

Words and Music by Graham Nash

Strum Pattern: 3, 4
Pick Pattern: 1, 3

Intro
Moderately slow, in 2

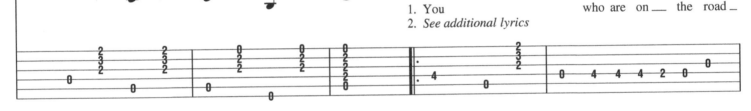

Verse

1. You who are on ___ the road ___
2. *See additional lyrics*

___ must have a code ___ that ___ you can live by.

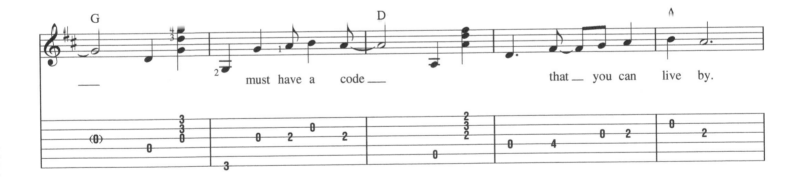

And so be - come ___ your - self be - cause the past ___

is just a good - bye. Teach

your {chil - dren / par - ents} well. Their {fa - ther's / chil - dren's} hell

{did / will} slow - ly go ___ by. And feed them on ___ your

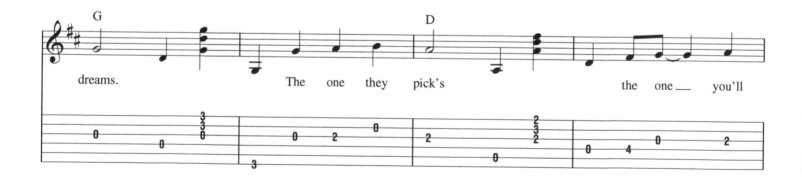

dreams. The one they pick's the one ___ you'll

know by. Don't you ev - er ask ___ them

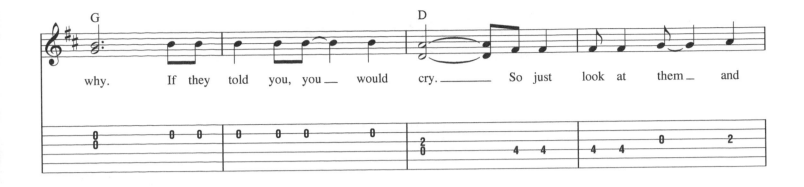

why.   If   they   told   you, you — would   cry. _____ So just   look   at   them — and

sigh _____   and   know   they   love ____ you.

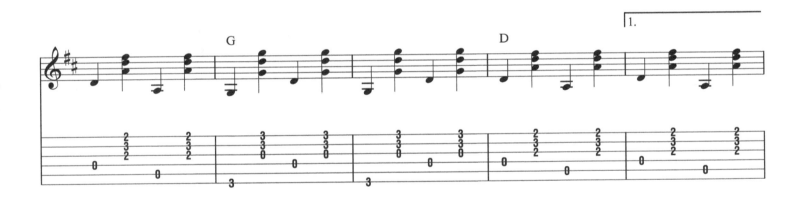

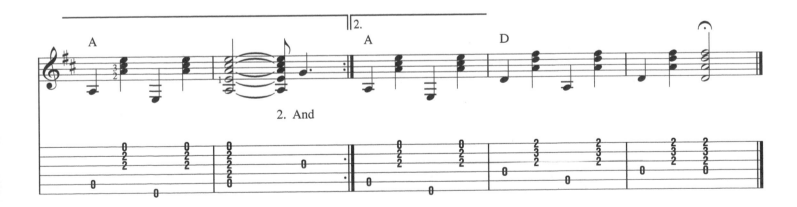

2. And

Additional Lyrics

2. And you of the tender years
   Can't know the fears that your elders grew by.
   And so, please help them with your youth.
   They seek the truth before they can die.

Southern Cross

Words and Music by Stephen Stills, Richard Curtis and Michael Curtis

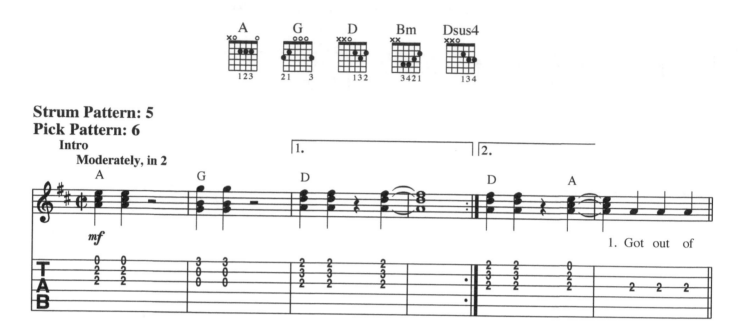

Strum Pattern: 5
Pick Pattern: 6

Intro
Moderately, in 2

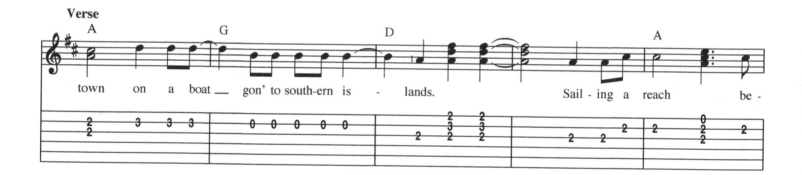

Verse

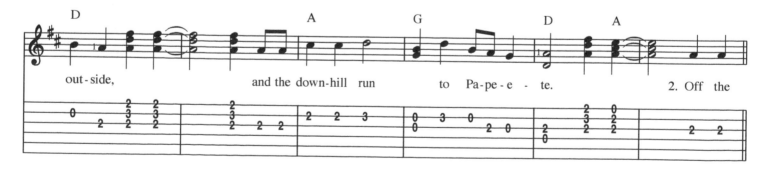

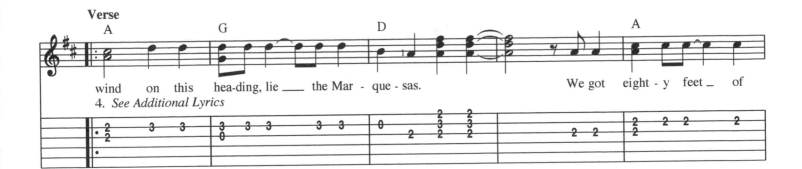

Verse

wind on this hea-ding, lie ___ the Mar - que - sas.
4. *See Additional Lyrics*

We got eight - y feet ___ of

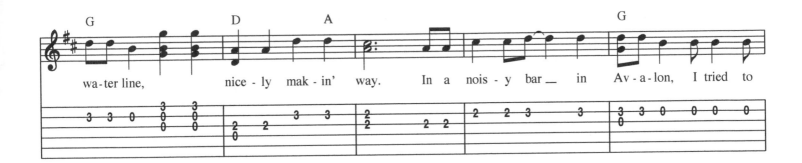

wa-ter line, nice - ly mak - in' way. In a nois - y bar ___ in Av - a - lon, I tried to

call you, but on the mid-night watch I re - al - ized why twice you ran a - way. ___

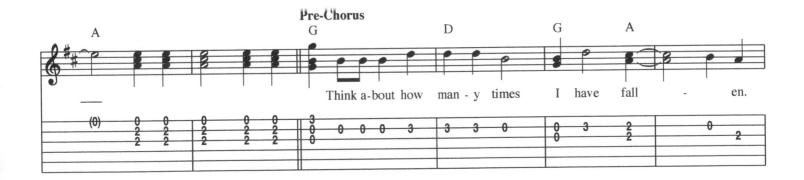

Pre-Chorus

Think a-bout how man - y times I have fall - en.

Spir - its are us - in' me; larg - er voic - es call - in'. What heav-en brought

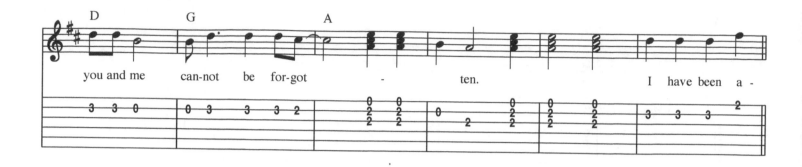

you and me can-not be for-got - ten. I have been a -

Chorus

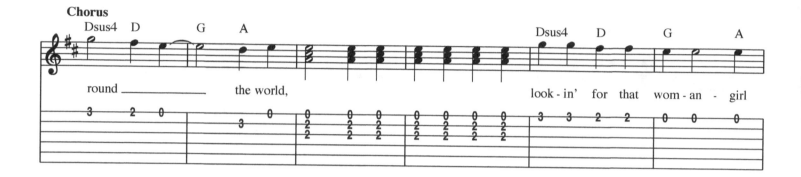

round _____ the world, look - in' for that wom - an - girl

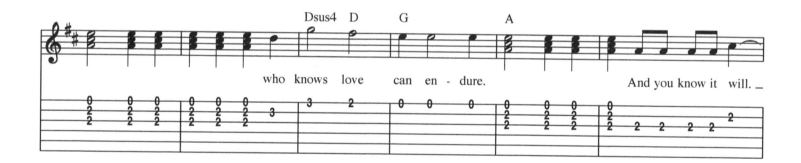

who knows love can en - dure. And you know it will. _

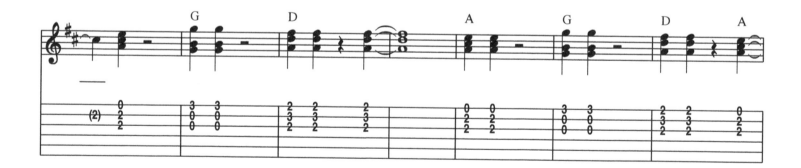

Verse

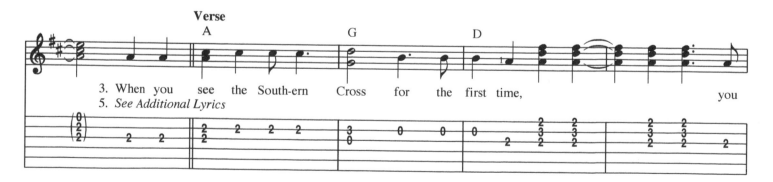

3. When you see the South-ern Cross for the first time, you
5. *See Additional Lyrics*

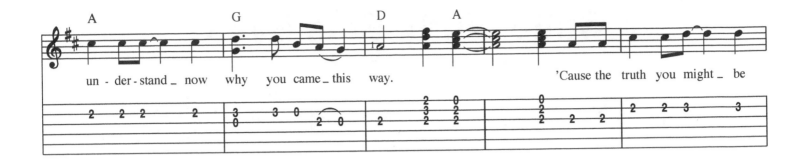

un - der - stand _ now why you came _ this way.　'Cause the truth you might _ be

run-nin' from is so small,　but it's as big as the prom-ise, —　the

prom-ise of a com-in' day.　4. So I'm　in the South-ern Cross.

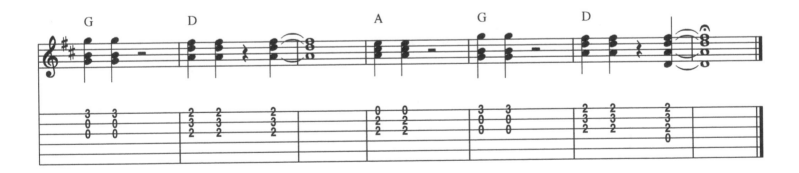

Additional Lyrics

4. So I'm sailing for tomorrow. My dreams are a-dying.
   And my love is an anchor tied to you, tied with a silver chain.
   I have my ship, and all her flags are a-flying.
   She is all that I have left, and music is her name.

5. So we cheated and we lied and we tested.
   And we never failed to fail; it was the easiest thing to do.
   You will survive being bested.
   Somebody fine will come along, make me forget about loving you
   In the Southern Cross.

Suite: Judy Blue Eyes

Words and Music by Stephen Stills

Strum Pattern: 2
Pick Pattern: 4

Intro
Moderately fast

mf

1. It's

%Verse

get-ting to the point where I'm no ___ fun an - y - more.
2., 4. *See additional lyrics*

I am ___ sor - ry. Some-times it hurts ___ so

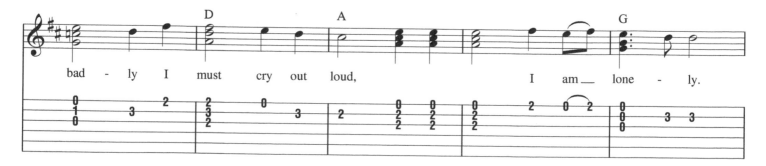

bad - ly I must cry out loud, I am ___ lone - ly.

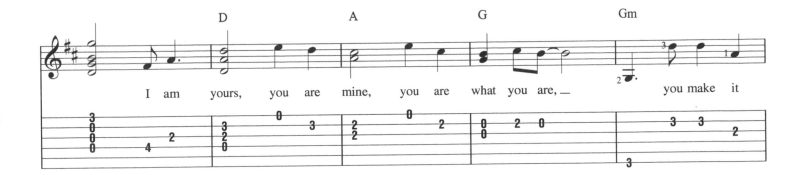

I am yours, you are mine, you are what you are, ___ you make it

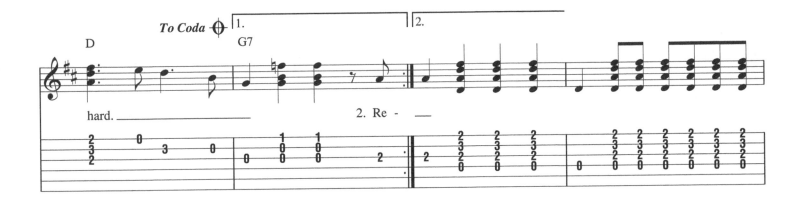

hard. _____ 2. Re - ___

3. Tear - ing your - self ___ a - way from me

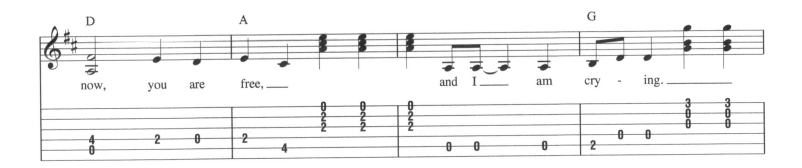

now, you are free, ___ and I ___ am cry - ing. _____

This does not mean ___ I don't love you, I do, that's for -

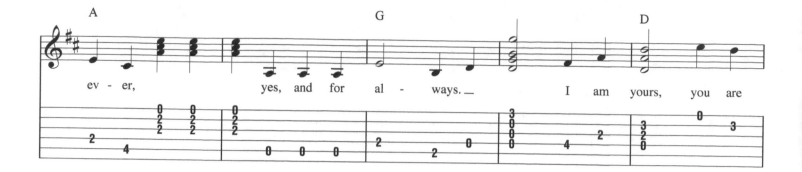

ev - er,   yes, and for al - ways. ___   I am yours, you are

mine,   you are what you are. _____   You make it   hard. _____

D.S. al Coda

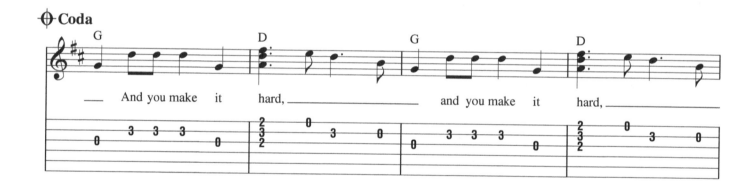

⊕**Coda**

___ And you make it hard, _____   and you make it hard, _____

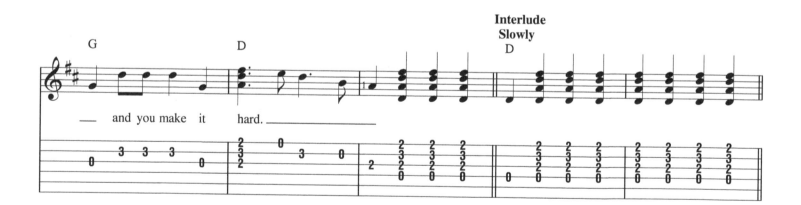

___ and you make it hard. _____

Interlude
Slowly

Bridge

Fri - day   eve - ning, _____   Sun - day in the af - ter - noon,
Tues - day morn - ing, _____   please _ be gone, I'm tired of you. _

What have you got to lose?

Can I tell it like it is? Lis-ten to me ba - by.

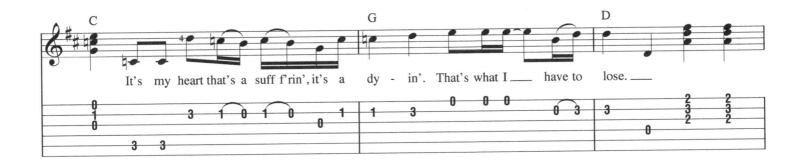

It's my heart that's a suff f'rin', it's a dy - in'. That's what I have to lose.

I've got an an - swer I'm going to
Will you come see me Thurs - days and

fly a - way.
Sat - ur - days?

What have I got to lose?
What have you got to lose?

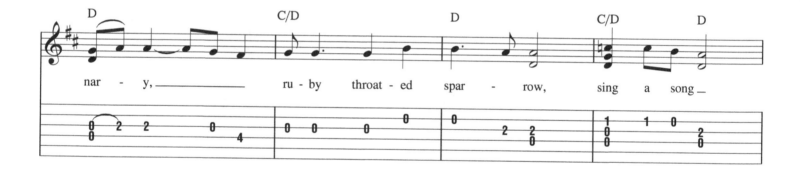

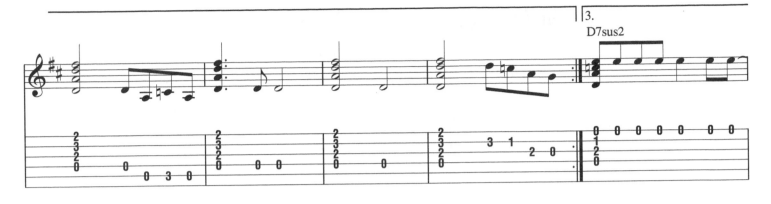

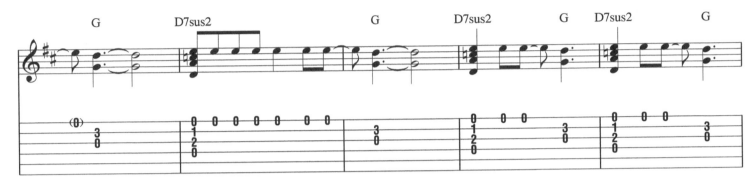

Additional Lyrics

2. Remember what we've said and done and felt about each other.
   Oh babe, have mercy.
   Don't let the past remind us of what we are not now.
   I am not dreaming.
   I am yours, you are mine, you are what you are.
   You make it hard.

4. Something inside is telling me that I've got your secret.
   Are you still list'ning?
   Fear is the lock and laughter the key to your heart.
   And I love you.
   I am yours, you are mine, you are what you are.
   You make it hard.
   And you make it hard.

6. Voices of the angels,
   Ring around the moonlight,
   Asking me, said she's so free,
   "How can you catch the sparrow?"

7. Lacy, lilting lyric,
   Losing love, lamenting,
   Change my life, make it right,
   Be my lady.

Wasted on the Way

Words and Music by Graham Nash

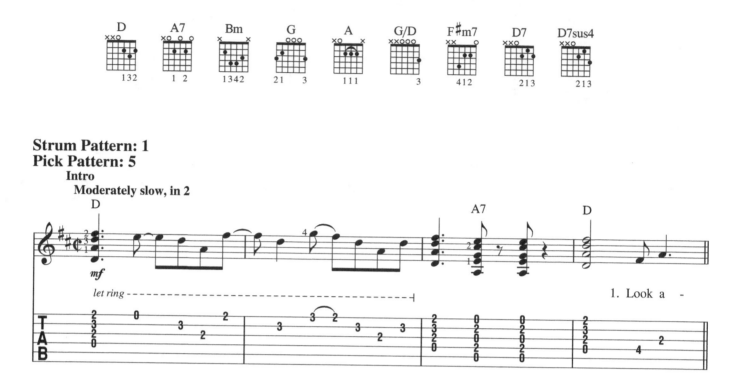

Strum Pattern: 1
Pick Pattern: 5

Intro

Moderately slow, in 2

mf

let ring

1. Look a -

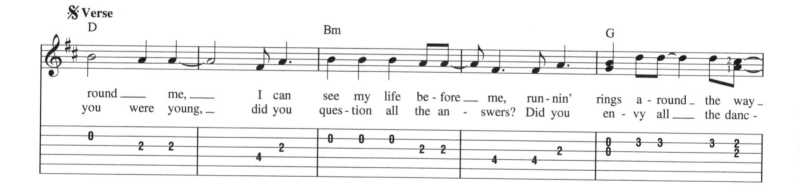

Verse

round ___ me, ___ I can see my life be - fore ___ me, run - nin' rings a - round __ the way __
you were young, _ did you ques - tion all the an - swers? Did you en - vy all __ the danc -

__ it used to be. __ I am old - er now, __ I have more than what I want -
- ers who had all the nerve? _ Look a - round you now, __ you must go for what you want -

*2nd time, substitute G

**2nd time, substitute D

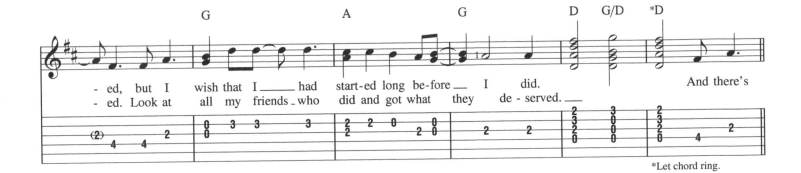

*Let chord ring.

Chorus

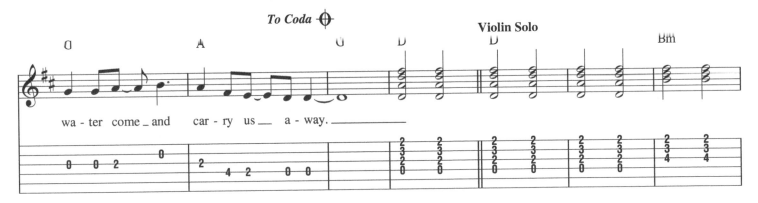

F#m7 D7 D7sus4 G A D Bm

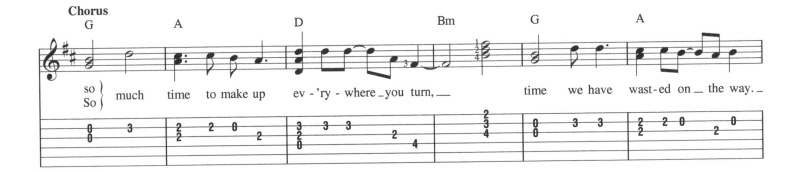

**2nd time, substitute D

To Coda

Violin Solo

 Coda

D.S. al Coda

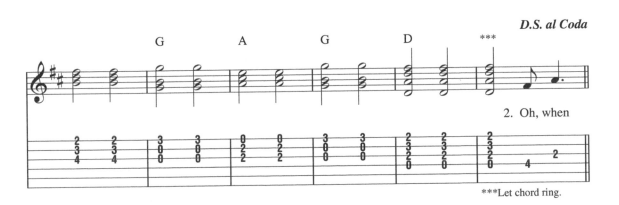

2. Oh, when

***Let chord ring.

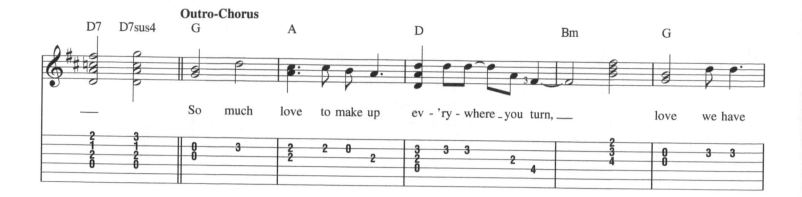

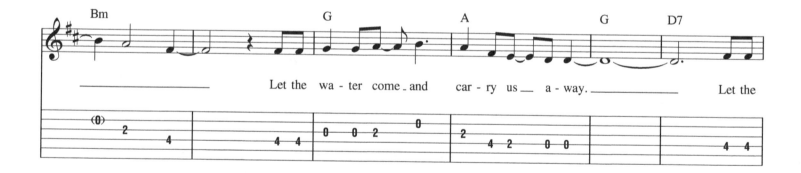

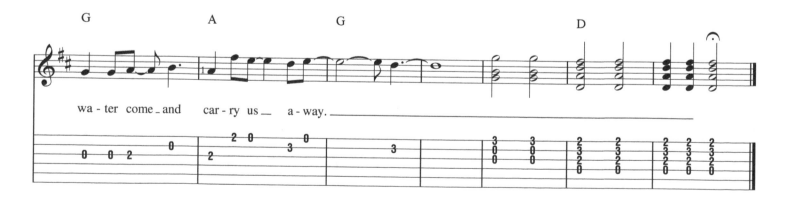

EASY GUITAR
WITH NOTES & TAB

This series features simplified arrangements with notes, tab, chord charts, and strum and pick patterns.

MIXED FOLIOS

00702287 Acoustic $14.99	00702225 Country Hits of '06–'07 ....$12.95	00702271 1960s Rock $14.99
00702002 Acoustic Rock Hits for Easy Guitar $12.95	00702085 Disney Movie Hits $12.95	00702270 1970s Rock $14.99
00702166 All-Time Best Guitar Collection.............$19.99	00702257 Easy Acoustic Guitar Songs $14.99	00702269 1980s Rock $14.99
00699665 Beatles Best $12.95	00702280 Easy Guitar Tab White Pages $29.99	00702268 1990s Rock $14.99
00702232 Best Acoustic Songs for Easy Guitar $12.99	00702212 Essential Christmas $9.95	00109725 Once $14.99
00702233 Best Hard Rock Songs $14.99	00702041 Favorite Hymns for Easy Guitar $9.95	00702187 Selections from
00703055 The Big Book of Nursery Rhymes	00702281 4 Chord Rock $9.99	O Brother Where Art Thou? $12.95
& Children's Songs $14.99	00702286 Glee $16.99	00702178 100 Songs for Kids..............$12.95
00322179 The Big Easy Book	00702174 God Bless America®	00702515 Pirates of the Caribbean $12.99
of Classic Rock Guitar $24.95	& Other Songs for a Better Nation $8.95	00702125 Praise and Worship for Guitar $9.95
00698978 Big Christmas Collection..............$16.95	00699374 Gospel Favorites..................$14.95	00702155 Rock Hits for Guitar.............$9.95
00702394 Bluegrass Songs for Easy Guitar $12.99	00702160 The Great American Country Songbook..$15.99	00702110 The Sound of Music.............$9.99
00703387 Celtic Classics $14.99	00702050 Great Classical Themes for Easy Guitar.....$6.95	00702285 Southern Rock Hits $12.99
00702149 Children's Christian Songbook..........$7.95	00702131 Great Country Hits of the '90s................$8.95	00702866 Theme Music $12.99
00702237 Christian Acoustic Favorites $12.95	00702116 Greatest Hymns for Guitar $8.95	00702124 Today's Christian Rock – 2nd Edition $9.95
00702028 Christmas Classics $7.95	00702130 The Groovy Years.................$9.95	00702220 Today's Country Hits $9.95
00101779 Christmas Guitar $14.99	00702184 Guitar Instrumentals $9.95	00702198 Today's Hits for Guitar $9.95
00702185 Christmas Hits...................$9.95	00702046 Hits of the '70s for Easy Guitar $8.95	00702217 Top Christian Hits $12.95
00702016 Classic Blues for Easy Guitar $12.95	00702273 Irish Songs $12.99	00702235 Top Christian Hits of '07–'08...........$14.95
00702141 Classic Rock $8.95	00702275 Jazz Favorites for Easy Guitar $14.99	00103626 Top Hits of 2012 ....$14.99
00702203 CMT's 100 Greatest Country Songs $27.95	00702274 Jazz Standards for Easy Guitar $14.99	00702556 Top Hits of 2011 ....$14.99
00702283 The Contemporary	00702162 Jumbo Easy Guitar Songbook $19.95	00702294 Top Worship Hits $14.99
Christian Collection $16.99	00702258 Legends of Rock $14.99	00702206 Very Best of Rock $9.95
00702006 Contemporary Christian Favorites..........$9.95	00702261 Modern Worship Hits $14.99	00702255 VH1's 100 Greatest Hard Rock Songs $27.99
00702239 Country Classics for Easy Guitar $19.99	00702189 MTV's 100 Greatest Pop Songs $24.95	00702175 VH1's 100 Greatest Songs
00702282 Country Hits of 2009–2010 ....$14.99	00702272 1950s Rock $14.99	of Rock and Roll...............$24.95
00702240 Country Hits of 2007–2008 ....$12.95		00702253 Wicked $12.99

ARTIST COLLECTIONS

00702267 AC/DC for Easy Guitar...................$15.99	00702190 Best of Pat Green $19.95	00699415 Best of Queen for Guitar.............$14.99
00702598 Adele for Easy Guitar $14.99	00702136 Best of Merle Haggard.................$12.99	00109279 Best of R.E.M. $14.99
00702001 Best of Aerosmith $16.95	00702247 Hannah Montana $16.95	00702208 Red Hot Chili Peppers — Greatest Hits..$19.95
00702040 Best of the Allman Brothers...........$14.99	00702244 Hannah Montana 2/Meet Miley Cyrus.......$16.95	00702093 Rolling Stones Collection $17.95
00702865 J.S. Bach for Easy Guitar $12.99	00702227 Jimi Hendrix — Smash Hits...............$14.99	00702092 Best of the Rolling Stones $14.99
00702169 Best of The Beach Boys $12.99	00702288 Best of Hillsong United $12.99	00702196 Best of Bob Seger $12.95
00702292 The Beatles — 1 ....$19.99	00702236 Best of Antonio Carlos Jobim $12.95	00702252 Frank Sinatra — Nothing But the Best ..$12.99
00702201 The Essential Black Sabbath $12.95	00702245 Elton John —	00702010 Best of Rod Stewart...................$14.95
00702140 Best of Brooks & Dunn.................$10.95	Greatest Hits 1970–2002 ....$14.99	00702049 Best of George Strait................$12.95
02501615 Zac Brown Band — The Foundation $16.99	00702204 Robert Johnson $9.95	00702259 Taylor Swift for Easy Guitar $14.99
02501621 Zac Brown Band —	00702277 Best of Jonas Brothers $14.99	00115960 Taylor Swift — Red $16.99
You Get What You Give $16.99	00702234 Selections from Toby Keith —	00702290 Taylor Swift — Speak Now $14.99
00702095 Best of Mariah Carey $12.95	35 Biggest Hits $12.95	00702223 Chris Tomlin — Arriving $12.95
00702043 Best of Johnny Cash $16.99	00702003 Kiss $9.95	00702262 Chris Tomlin Collection $14.99
00702033 Best of Steven Curtis Chapman $14.95	00702193 Best of Jennifer Knapp $12.95	00702226 Chris Tomlin — See the Morning..........$12.95
00702291 Very Best of Coldplay $12.99	00702097 John Lennon — Imagine...............$9.95	00702132 Shania Twain — Greatest Hits $10.95
00702263 Best of Casting Crowns $12.99	00702216 Lynyrd Skynyrd $15.99	00702427 U2 — 18 Singles $14.99
00702090 Eric Clapton's Best....................$10.95	00702182 The Essential Bob Marley $12.95	00702108 Best of Stevie Ray Vaughan $10.95
00702086 Eric Clapton —	00702346 Bruno Mars —	00702123 Best of Hank Williams............$12.95
from the Album Unplugged...........$10.95	Doo-Wops & Hooligans $12.99	00702111 Stevie Wonder — Guitar Collection..........$9.95
00702202 The Essential Eric Clapton $12.95	00702248 Paul McCartney — All the Best $14.99	00702228 Neil Young — Greatest Hits $15.99
00702250 blink-182 — Greatest Hits $12.99	00702129 Songs of Sarah McLachlan.................$12.95	00702188 Essential ZZ Top $10.95
00702053 Best of Patsy Cline....................$10.95	02501316 Metallica — Death Magnetic $15.95	
00702229 The Very Best of	00702209 Steve Miller Band —	
Creedence Clearwater Revival.................$14.99	Young Hearts (Greatest Hits)...............$12.95	
00702145 Best of Jim Croce....................$12.99	00702096 Best of Nirvana $14.95	
00702278 Crosby, Stills & Nash $12.99	00702211 The Offspring — Greatest Hits $12.95	
00702219 David Crowder*Band Collection $12.95	00702030 Best of Roy Orbison $12.95	
00702122 The Doors for Easy Guitar $12.99	00702144 Best of Ozzy Osbourne................$14.99	
00702276 Fleetwood Mac —	00702279 Tom Petty $12.99	
Easy Guitar Collection $12.99	00702139 Elvis Country Favorites...........$9.95	
00702099 Best of Amy Grant..................$9.95	00702293 The Very Best of Prince $12.99	

HAL•LEONARD® CORPORATION

7777 W. BLUEMOUND RD. P.O. BOX 13819 MILWAUKEE, WI 53213

Visit Hal Leonard online at
www.halleonard.com

0113

HAL•LEONARD GUITAR PLAY•ALONG®

This series will help you play your favorite songs quickly and easily. Just follow the tab and listen to the CD to the hear how the guitar should sound, and then play along using the separate backing tracks. Mac or PC users can also slow down the tempo without changing pitch by using the CD in their computer. The melody and lyrics are included in the book so that you can sing or simply follow along.

INCLUDES TAB

VOL. 1 – ROCK	00699570 / $16.99	
VOL. 2 – ACOUSTIC	00699569 / $16.95	
VOL. 3 – HARD ROCK	00699573 / $16.95	
VOL. 4 – POP/ROCK	00699571 / $16.99	
VOL. 5 – MODERN ROCK	00699574 / $16.99	
VOL. 6 – '90s ROCK	00699572 / $16.99	
VOL. 7 – BLUES	00699575 / $16.95	
VOL. 8 – ROCK	00699585 / $14.99	
VOL. 9 – PUNK ROCK	00699576 / $14.95	
VOL. 10 – ACOUSTIC	00699586 / $16.95	
VOL. 11 – EARLY ROCK	00699579 / $14.95	
VOL. 12 – POP/ROCK	00699587 / $14.95	
VOL. 13 – FOLK ROCK	00699581 / $15.99	
VOL. 14 – BLUES ROCK	00699582 / $16.95	
VOL. 15 – R&B	00699583 / $14.95	
VOL. 16 – JAZZ	00699584 / $15.95	
VOL. 17 – COUNTRY	00699588 / $15.95	
VOL. 18 – ACOUSTIC ROCK	00699577 / $15.95	
VOL. 19 – SOUL	00699578 / $14.99	
VOL. 20 – ROCKABILLY	00699580 / $14.95	
VOL. 21 – YULETIDE	00699602 / $14.95	
VOL. 22 – CHRISTMAS	00699600 / $15.95	
VOL. 23 – SURF	00699635 / $14.95	
VOL. 24 – ERIC CLAPTON	00699649 / $17.99	
VOL. 25 – LENNON & McCARTNEY	00699642 / $16.99	
VOL. 26 – ELVIS PRESLEY	00699643 / $14.95	
VOL. 27 – DAVID LEE ROTH	00699645 / $16.95	
VOL. 28 – GREG KOCH	00699646 / $14.95	
VOL. 29 – BOB SEGER	00699647 / $15.99	
VOL. 30 – KISS	00699644 / $16.99	
VOL. 31 – CHRISTMAS HITS	00699652 / $14.95	
VOL. 32 – THE OFFSPRING	00699653 / $14.95	
VOL. 33 – ACOUSTIC CLASSICS	00699656 / $16.95	
VOL. 34 – CLASSIC ROCK	00699658 / $16.95	
VOL. 35 – HAIR METAL	00699660 / $16.95	
VOL. 36 – SOUTHERN ROCK	00699661 / $16.95	
VOL. 37 – ACOUSTIC METAL	00699662 / $16.95	
VOL. 38 – BLUES	00699663 / $16.95	
VOL. 39 – '80s METAL	00699664 / $16.99	
VOL. 40 – INCUBUS	00699668 / $17.95	
VOL. 41 – ERIC CLAPTON	00699669 / $16.95	
VOL. 42 – 2000s ROCK	00699670 / $16.99	
VOL. 43 – LYNYRD SKYNYRD	00699681 / $17.95	
VOL. 44 – JAZZ	00699689 / $14.99	
VOL. 45 – TV THEMES	00699718 / $14.95	
VOL. 46 – MAINSTREAM ROCK	00699722 / $16.95	
VOL. 47 – HENDRIX SMASH HITS	00699723 / $19.95	
VOL. 48 – AEROSMITH CLASSICS	00699724 / $17.99	
VOL. 49 – STEVIE RAY VAUGHAN	00699725 / $17.99	
VOL. 51 – ALTERNATIVE '90s	00699727 / $14.99	
VOL. 52 – FUNK	00699728 / $14.95	

VOL. 53 – DISCO	00699729 / $14.99	
VOL. 54 – HEAVY METAL	00699730 / $14.95	
VOL. 55 – POP METAL	00699731 / $14.95	
VOL. 56 – FOO FIGHTERS	00699749 / $15.99	
VOL. 57 – SYSTEM OF A DOWN	00699751 / $14.95	
VOL. 58 – BLINK-182	00699772 / $14.95	
VOL. 60 – 3 DOORS DOWN	00699774 / $14.95	
VOL. 61 – SLIPKNOT	00699775 / $16.99	
VOL. 62 – CHRISTMAS CAROLS	00699798 / $12.95	
VOL. 63 – CREEDENCE CLEARWATER REVIVAL	00699802 / $16.99	
VOL. 64 – THE ULTIMATE OZZY OSBOURNE	00699803 / $16.99	
VOL. 65 – THE DOORS	00699806 / $16.99	
VOL. 66 – THE ROLLING STONES	00699807 / $16.95	
VOL. 67 – BLACK SABBATH	00699808 / $16.99	
VOL. 68 – PINK FLOYD – DARK SIDE OF THE MOON	00699809 / $16.99	
VOL. 69 – ACOUSTIC FAVORITES	00699810 / $14.95	
VOL. 70 – OZZY OSBOURNE	00699805 / $16.99	
VOL. 71 – CHRISTIAN ROCK	00699824 / $14.95	
VOL. 72 – ACOUSTIC '90s	00699827 / $14.95	
VOL. 73 – BLUESY ROCK	00699829 / $16.99	
VOL. 74 – PAUL BALOCHE	00699831 / $14.95	
VOL. 75 – TOM PETTY	00699882 / $16.99	
VOL. 76 – COUNTRY HITS	00699884 / $14.95	
VOL. 77 – BLUEGRASS	00699910 / $14.99	
VOL. 78 – NIRVANA	00700132 / $16.99	
VOL. 79 – NEIL YOUNG	00700133 / $24.99	
VOL. 80 – ACOUSTIC ANTHOLOGY	00700175 / $19.95	
VOL. 81 – ROCK ANTHOLOGY	00700176 / $22.99	
VOL. 82 – EASY SONGS	00700177 / $12.99	
VOL. 83 – THREE CHORD SONGS	00700178 / $16.99	
VOL. 84 – STEELY DAN	00700200 / $16.99	
VOL. 85 – THE POLICE	00700269 / $16.99	
VOL. 86 – BOSTON	00700465 / $16.99	
VOL. 87 – ACOUSTIC WOMEN	00700763 / $14.99	
VOL. 88 – GRUNGE	00700467 / $16.99	
VOL. 90 – CLASSICAL POP	00700469 / $14.99	
VOL. 91 – BLUES INSTRUMENTALS	00700505 / $14.99	
VOL. 92 – EARLY ROCK INSTRUMENTALS	00700506 / $14.99	
VOL. 93 – ROCK INSTRUMENTALS	00700507 / $16.99	
VOL. 95 – BLUES CLASSICS	00700509 / $14.99	
VOL. 96 – THIRD DAY	00700560 / $14.95	
VOL. 97 – ROCK BAND	00700703 / $14.99	
VOL. 98 – ROCK BAND	00700704 / $14.95	
VOL. 99 – ZZ TOP	00700762 / $16.99	
VOL. 100 – B.B. KING	00700466 / $16.99	
VOL. 101 – SONGS FOR BEGINNERS	00701917 / $14.99	
VOL. 102 – CLASSIC PUNK	00700769 / $14.99	
VOL. 103 – SWITCHFOOT	00700773 / $16.99	

VOL. 104 – DUANE ALLMAN	00700846 / $16.99	
VOL. 106 – WEEZER	00700958 / $14.99	
VOL. 107 – CREAM	00701069 / $16.99	
VOL. 108 – THE WHO	00701053 / $16.99	
VOL. 109 – STEVE MILLER	00701054 / $14.99	
VOL. 111 – JOHN MELLENCAMP	00701056 / $14.99	
VOL. 112 – QUEEN	00701052 / $16.99	
VOL. 113 – JIM CROCE	00701058 / $15.99	
VOL. 114 – BON JOVI	00701060 / $14.99	
VOL. 115 – JOHNNY CASH	00701070 / $16.99	
VOL. 116 – THE VENTURES	00701124 / $14.99	
VOL. 118 – ERIC JOHNSON	00701353 / $14.99	
VOL. 119 – AC/DC CLASSICS	00701356 / $17.99	
VOL. 120 – PROGRESSIVE ROCK	00701457 / $14.99	
VOL. 121 – U2	00701508 / $16.99	
VOL. 123 – LENNON & McCARTNEY ACOUSTIC	00701614 / $16.99	
VOL. 124 – MODERN WORSHIP	00701629 / $14.99	
VOL. 125 – JEFF BECK	00701687 / $16.99	
VOL. 126 – BOB MARLEY	00701701 / $16.99	
VOL. 127 – 1970s ROCK	00701739 / $14.99	
VOL. 128 – 1960s ROCK	00701740 / $14.99	
VOL. 129 – MEGADETH	00701741 / $16.99	
VOL. 131 – 1990s ROCK	00701743 / $14.99	
VOL. 132 – COUNTRY ROCK	00701757 / $15.99	
VOL. 133 – TAYLOR SWIFT	00701894 / $16.99	
VOL. 134 – AVENGED SEVENFOLD	00701906 / $16.99	
VOL. 136 – GUITAR THEMES	00701922 / $14.99	
VOL. 138 – BLUEGRASS CLASSICS	00701967 / $14.99	
VOL. 139 – GARY MOORE	00702370 / $16.99	
VOL. 140 – MORE STEVIE RAY VAUGHAN	00702396 / $17.99	
VOL. 141 – ACOUSTIC HITS	00702401 / $16.99	
VOL. 142 – KINGS OF LEON	00702418 / $16.99	
VOL. 144 – DJANGO REINHARDT	00702531 / $16.99	
VOL. 145 – DEF LEPPARD	00702532 / $16.99	
VOL. 147 – SIMON & GARFUNKEL	14041591 / $16.99	
VOL. 149 – AC/DC HITS	14041593 / $17.99	
VOL. 150 – ZAKK WYLDE	02501717 / $16.99	
VOL. 153 – RED HOT CHILI PEPPERS	00702990 / $19.99	
VOL. 157 – FLEETWOOD MAC	00101382 / $16.99	
VOL. 158 – ULTIMATE CHRISTMAS	00101889 / $14.99	
VOL. 161 – THE EAGLES – ACOUSTIC	00102659 / $16.99	
VOL. 162 – THE EAGLES HITS	00102667 / $17.99	
VOL. 166 – MODERN BLUES	00700764 / $16.99	

Complete song lists available online.

Prices, contents, and availability subject to change without notice.

HAL•LEONARD® CORPORATION
7777 W. BLUEMOUND RD. P.O. BOX 13819 MILWAUKEE, WI 53213

www.halleonard.com

0113